Today the weather is sunny and warm. WomWom comes out of her burrow. The day is not hot now. It is a good time to explore.

Some days WomWom goes to the beach. It is not far from her burrow. WomWom is happy to be outside.

Some days are cold and rainy. WomWom stays in her burrow. She does not like the rain.

Some days are windy. WomWom does not like the wind. WomWom will get cold in the wind.

Some days there is no wind. WomWom walks to the rocks next to the sea. She looks at the calm water.

WomWom can see the clouds. The clouds are like a fog. It may rain soon. The rain helps the plants grow.

Some days it is very cold.
The rain may turn to snow.
Frozen rain is called snow.
The snow can melt to form water.

WomWom can see fluffy, white clouds. The clouds have different shapes today. What shapes can you see?

There are many different types of clouds. Some clouds are high in the sky and some are low.

WomWom eats grass outside when the weather is fine. She stays in the burrow when it is cold or rainy.

WomWom goes to her burrow when the weather changes. Some of the clouds are dark. It may rain soon.

WomWom looks at a rainbow in the sky. The rainbow is made by the sunlight. When did you see a rainbow?